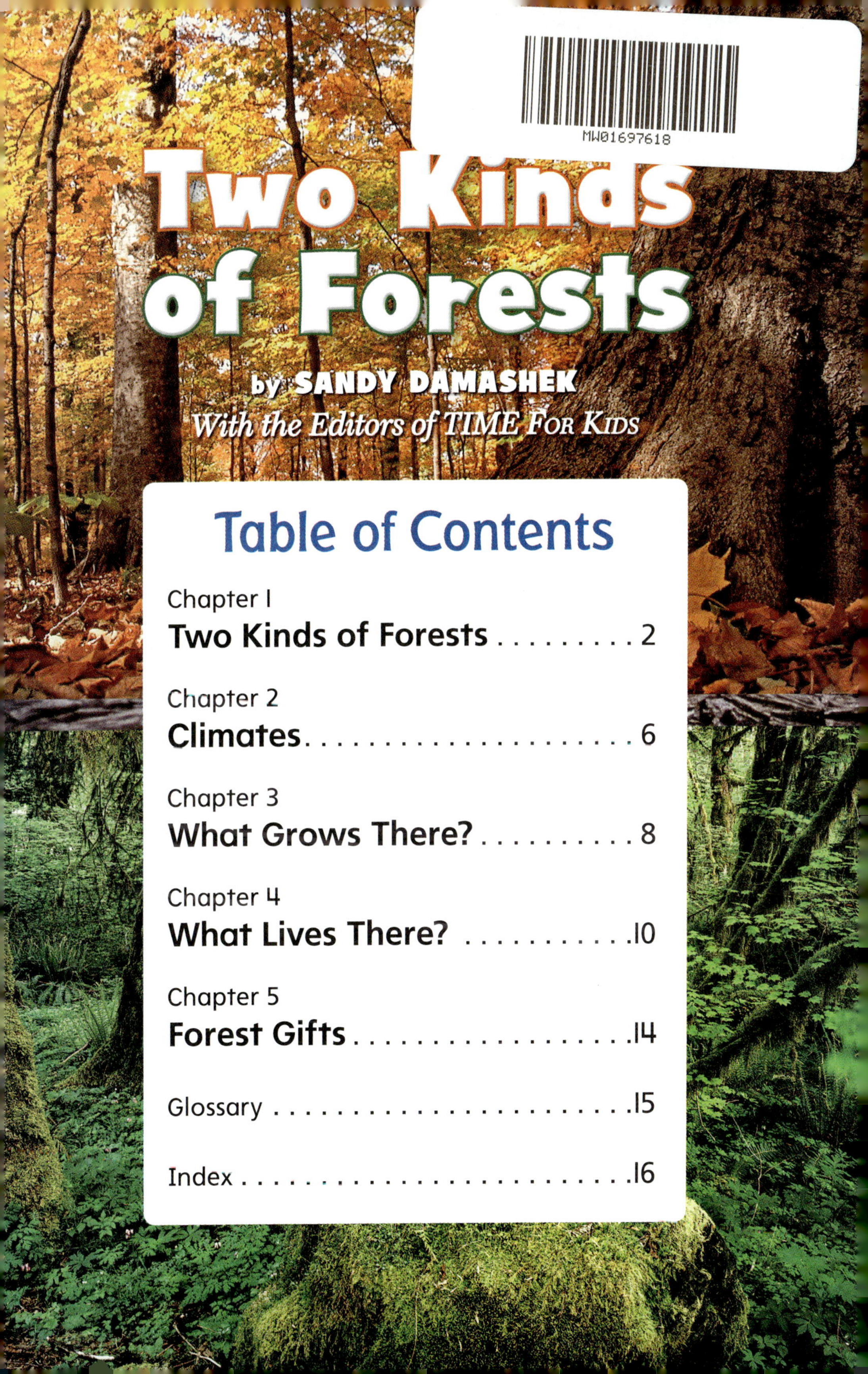

# Two Kinds of Forests

by SANDY DAMASHEK
*With the Editors of TIME For Kids*

## Table of Contents

Chapter 1

# Two Kinds of Forests

This is a woodland forest.

People build treehouses in the forest. You can build a treehouse in a **woodland forest** or in a **rain forest**.

This is a rain forest.

What is a woodland forest? What is a rain forest? Where are they? You will learn about these forests in this book.

When the weather gets cold, the trees in a woodland forest drop their leaves. We find rain forests in hot and rainy places. Where are these forests? Look at the map. We can learn from the map.

**Woodland Forests and Rain Forests of the World**

Look at the **equator** in the map. It is an imaginary line around the Earth. You can see it on this map. The map also shows the forests. Rain forests are near the equator. Woodland forests are far from it.

Chapter 2

# Climates

A woodland forest has snow in the winter.

A **climate** is the kind of weather in a place. Woodland forests and rain forests have different climates. Woodland forests grow in climates with sun and snow. They are hot in the summer and cold in the winter.

Rain forests grow in climates that are always hot and wet. It rains almost every day in a rain forest. Would you like to live in that climate?

A rain forest does not have winters. It is always hot.

Chapter 3

# What Grows There?

The weather changes a lot in a woodland forest. The trees change, too.

In summer, the trees have a lot of leaves. In fall, the leaves change color and fall down. In winter, the trees do not have many leaves. In spring, new leaves grow.

Plants grow all year in a rain forest.

You can find many different kinds of plants and trees growing in a rain forest. The weather is always hot and wet there. In that climate, the plants can grow all year.

Chapter 4

# What Lives There?

Porcupine

These animals live in a woodland forest.

Black bear cubs

Many animals live in a woodland forest. They find lots of food in the summer and fall. In winter, these animals cannot find much food.

Some animals, like squirrels, save food in summer and fall. They eat the food in winter. Bears **hibernate**, or sleep, all winter. Some birds **migrate**. They fly to warmer places for the winter.

Sloth

Toucan

Iguana

These animals live in a rain forest.

A rain forest has many animals. Maybe you know some of them. Some of the animals only live in rain forests!

Food grows all year in the hot, wet climate of the rain forest. Animals can always find food. They can live the same way all year.

Chapter 5

# Forest Gifts

Here are some things we get from woodland forests and rain forests. We use them every day.

**Woodland Forest**

| | |
|---|---|
| Apple |  |
| Blackberries |  |
| Maple syrup |  |
| Lumber |  |

**Rain Forest**

| | |
|---|---|
| Avocado |  |
| Banana |  |
| Chocolate |  |
| Coffee |  |

# Glossary

**climate** (KLYE-mit) the kind of weather in a place *(page 6)*

**equator** (i-KWAY-tuhr) the imaginary line around Earth *(page 5)*

**hibernate** (HYE-buhr-nayt) to sleep all winter *(page 11)*

**migrate** (MYE-grayt) to move from one place to another based on the seasons *(page 11)*

**rain forest** (RAYN FOR-ist) a thick forest where the weather is hot and rainy all year *(page 2)*

**woodland forest** (WUD-land FOR-ist) a forest where trees lose their leaves in the fall and grow new leaves in spring; the weather changes with the seasons *(page 2)*

# Index